C000224684

THE LOW-MAIN
GARDEN

PETER McHOY

HarperCollins*Publishers*

Products mentioned in this book

'Cutlass'	contains	dikegulac
'Bug Gun!'	contains	pyrethrum
'Lawnsman'		
Weed & Feed	contains	2, 4-D/dicamba
'Pathclear'	contains	diquat/paraquat/simazine
'Roseclear'	contains	bupirimate/pirimicarb/triforine*
'Weedol'	contains	diquat/paraquat

*Triforine is a product of Celamerck

Read the label before you buy; use pesticides safely

Editors Diana Brinton, Joey Chapter
Designer Joyce Mason
Picture research Moira McIlroy
Production Craig Chubb

First published in 1991 by
Harper Collins Publishers
London

**A CIP catalogue record for this book
is available from the British Library.**

ISBN 0-00-412602-5

Photoset by Litho Link Ltd, Welshpool, Powys, Wales
Printed and bound in Hong Kong by Dai Nippon Printing Company

Front cover: Low-maintenance border plants by the Harry Smith
Horticultural Collection
Back cover: Tulipa tarda by Derek Gould

CONTENTS

INTRODUCTION

There is a fine line between a garden being a pleasure and a problem, giving you seemingly endless work and worry. Fortunately, the solution to this dilemma is a simple one: if you plan and plant a low-maintenance garden, you will have all the pleasures of an attractive garden with the minimum of work. The aim of this book is to show how to achieve that goal.

There should be nothing second-rate about a low-maintenance garden. There's no reason why it can't be colourful and interesting – and look 'designed'.

Choosing plants Creating a low-maintenance garden does not simply mean paving large areas, or keeping plants to the minimum. It involves using plants and surfaces that tend to look after themselves with the minimum amount of care, and choosing plants that will thrive without having to be coaxed (or, equally important, constantly pruned or controlled in some other way). It's about achieving striking results with simple design features such as ornaments or interestingly-shaped shrubs, and maybe thinking seriously about abandoning some of those 'ingredients' of a good garden that we tend to take for granted. Digging up your lawn can take some courage, but it may be the kind of rethink that's necessary once you have considered the other options.

Initial planning A low-maintenance garden certainly saves time and effort in the long term, but you will probably have to put a lot of work into creating the garden in the first place, and this process may not be cheap. You will find plenty of ideas that can be adapted for those who wish to reduce the work in an established garden without resorting to redesigning it, but to cut the maintenance down drastically may call for some reconstruction or re-planting. You won't begrudge the initial effort that's involved once you begin to reap the benefits.

Low-maintenance approaches Some gardeners prefer to cut down on the chore of maintenance by investing in powered tools, but the suggestions that you'll find here assume that you're interested in saving time as much as effort.

Provided you can get some help with the initial transformation of your garden, a low-maintenance approach is also ideal for elderly or

LEFT The combination of gravel, flowering ground-cover plants and easily maintained border plants and climbers makes a delightful picture in a walled garden.

RIGHT A low-maintenance garden can be just as bright and full of bloom as any other — the initial planning is the most labour-intensive stage.

disabled gardeners, who love their plants and gardens but do not have the ability to cope with the routine maintenance of a garden.

As the illustrations in this book show, to opt for a labour-saving garden does not in any way make you an inferior gardener. By careful planning and suitable planting you can achieve a delightful and designed garden, and one of which you can be justly proud, even though you may only have a limited time to spend gardening.

ABOVE Paved areas softened by border planting can look attractive with minimal effort.

LEFT Imaginative planting in a paved garden.

SHRUBS AND CLIMBERS

Shrubs and climbers are the backbone plants for your garden, the ones that will help to give it shape and form. A garden without at least a few shrubs or climbers to provide an interesting background, and varied heights and depths, will almost certainly look stark and perhaps boring. The smaller the garden, the more important their role; the problem lies in selecting the most suitable plants from a bewildering choice.

Versatile slow-growing shrubs can enhance any garden and are indispensable for any low-maintenance planting scheme.

If you intend to create a low-maintenance garden, it is important to be very clear about the qualities that you require from a shrub. It's no use choosing simply those that take your fancy in a picture or in someone else's garden.

Plants to avoid Even the most vigorous shrubs are unlikely to require pruning or trimming more than a couple of times a year, and you may regard this as perfectly acceptable if it means having a plant that you want. But it is best to put the emphasis on easy-to-grow, compact or well-behaved shrubs that require very little pruning and that look good for a long period. It is wise to avoid plants with a short life; many brooms, for example, need replacing after a few years, while plants such as flowering currants and *Clematis montana* may quickly outgrow their space and require cutting back or removing.

Similarly, it is good sense to avoid any shrub that requires regular pruning, either to keep it compact or to keep it flowering well, and this includes such popular shrubs as forsythia, many dogwoods, and lilacs. This proviso also applies to certain climbers, such as the Russian vine *(Polygonum baldschuanicum)* and wisterias, which are very vigorous.

Criteria for selection Where possible, coloured or variegated foliage should be put to good use, and attractive flowers or fruit can be especially important, as you will probably be keeping the colourful but more labour-intensive annuals and herbaceous perennials normally found in a garden to a minimum.

You will find plenty of suggestions for useful low-maintenance shrubs in the Sixty of the Best chapter, but within a book of this size any list can recommend very few of the many that are available. Use the guidelines of what to avoid when choosing from among the many others that

you will find in garden centres and nurseries.

Don't overlook soil and aspect. A plant that does well in sun may struggle in shade, while plants that love an acid soil, such as rhododendrons and some heathers, will always struggle and need coaxing on an alkaline (chalky) soil. Special requirements have been noted in the plant lists, but there's a lot to be said for concentrating on those shrubs and climbers that grow well in most soils and situations.

Examples of good low-maintenance shrubs are the laurustinus *(Viburnum tinus)*, camellias and yuccas. The first of these makes an evergreen mound or pyramid that doesn't need pruning, and flowers from November or earlier through to March and beyond. Camellias are also evergreen, but will compete with any border flower for impact, and the eye-catching hardy yuccas produce huge spikes of big white bells.

ABOVE LEFT A colourful mixture of compact shrubs. Check aspect and soil before deciding which types to plant.

LEFT Yuccas are perfect as a focal point and can produce stunning spikes of flowers in good conditions.

ROSES AND HARDY PERENNIALS

Roses and herbaceous perennials are frequently regarded as labour-intensive plants, unsuitable for a low-maintenance garden, and this is true of most of them. Fortunately, there are roses and border perennials that are relatively trouble-free, so you don't have to miss out on these popular groups of plants; you just have to be selective.

For some gardeners, a garden simply isn't a proper garden without a rose. Unfortunately, roses are generally very demanding – they require regular pruning to produce abundant flowers; they benefit from feeding, and both pests and diseases seem as attracted by them as gardeners. It's best to forget the hybrid tea (large-flowered bush) and floribunda (cluster-flowered bush) roses, along with climbers and ramblers. Concentrate on the so-called shrub roses, which are less demanding about pruning (and some are more resistant to disease and other problems). There are singles and doubles; many are highly scented, and they are usually between 1m and 2m (3ft and 6ft) high.

'Ballerina' is an excellent variety, suitable for the herbaceous border as well as the rose bed. It produces masses of fragrant pink and white flowers, which appear over a long period. 'Cécile Brunner' (also known as the sweetheart rose) is also worth finding space for – it has small pink flowers and should not exceed 1m (3ft). Another short-list variety is the single pink, very fragrant 'Frau Dagmar Hartopp'. This flowers for a long period, has large red hips, is more disease-resistant than many roses, and will grow almost anywhere.

Border plants The main problem with herbaceous border plants is that the bare ground left when they die down is an invitation for weeds to colonize, and within a year or two the plants will probably require lifting and dividing. A degree of replanting is also usually necessary to make up for winter losses. Staking is the other major problem –

'Frau Dagmar Hartopp' is a delightfully scented rose that requires very little attention; it produces attractive red hips as well as having a long flowering season.

ABOVE A striking border display of *Kniphofia uvaria* 'Maxima'.

RIGHT *Hemerocallis* 'Apricot'. Day lilies are ideal for providing trouble-free colour in a border.

some of the big and beautiful plants, such as oriental poppies and achilleas, really need some support.

It is best to avoid the herbaceous and mixed borders, but you can use suitable herbaceous plants that don't require staking in other parts of the garden. Try a single plant of bear's breeches *(Acanthus spinosus)* as a focal-point plant, perhaps at the base of some steps; position a big bold clump of red hot pokers *(Kniphofia)* in front of shrubs or as a solitary specimen; make a small border of day lilies *(Hemerocallis)*, leaving them to form dense clumps, or plant an edging of the grey-blue grass *Festuca glauca*.

Ground cover Some hardy border plants can also be used as ground cover (see p.18). One of the finest, because it's evergreen and also very decorative in flower, is elephant ears *(Bergenia)*. There are several good species and varieties, all of which will grow in sun or shade, are excellent at suppressing weeds, and can be left to their own devices for years.

Others are worth including in a low-maintenance garden because they multiply slowly, suppress weeds, and are generally tough. *Liriope muscari* is one, and as a bonus is evergreen and produces its blue flower spikes in autumn when many flowers have died.

A herbaceous border If you feel that you must have a border of herbaceous plants, make it a small one, perhaps an island bed with some tall plants in the middle and smaller ones around the edge. Use plenty of carpeters around the edge of the bed to suppress weeds, and allow these plants to creep among the taller ones if possible – this will keep weeding to a minimum. There will be a time of the year when a bed like this will look at least a little bedraggled, and if you like a garden that looks neat and tidy at all times, you may prefer to use a mulch between the plants (see p. 26).

Choosing plants For your herbaceous bed, choose plants that require no staking. Avoid any that self-seed readily – plants such as fennel produce hundreds of seedlings that have to be weeded out each year. Similarly, you do not want plants that will spread too vigorously, but on the other hand it is useful to have some that will form large clumps if left to their own devices for a number of years.

Some alpines can also be used at the front of a border, especially carpeters such as bugle (*Ajuga reptans*), which retains its foliage for most of the year and usually smothers weeds. Perennial candytuft (*Iberis sempervirens*) is another rock garden plant that's worth including – it's evergreen, attractive in flower, and well behaved.

Edging Perennials are useful for edging beds and borders, but it is wise to use only those that are well behaved: those that are vigorous enough to thrive without much care yet not so vigorous or lax in habit that they need constant cutting back, and that won't be so prolific that they become a 'weed' problem.

BELOW *Veronica spicata* will thrive for many years with minimal care. The cultivar shown here is 'Red Fox'.

BOTTOM The creamy blooms of *Helleborus niger,* the Christmas rose, add interest to a garden in winter.

It is best to avoid the more rampant spreaders and free-seeders, such as *Lamium maculatum*, as they will need regular attention to keep them in check. Also avoid certain of the sedums, especially *S. acre* – it is sometimes sold as a carpeter or edging plant, but it will become a weed that is difficult to eliminate from the garden.

Choose plants with a long period of interest. It makes sense to place the emphasis on foliage plants for edging, though some, such as *Dianthus* (carnations and pinks), have pretty flowers and fragrance as well as long-lasting grey foliage. The old variety of pink called 'Doris' is still one of the finest that you can plant. *Nepeta* (catmint) also combines good foliage, fragrance (this time the leaves) and good, long-lasting flowers.

For a taller edging, some of the artemesias are very effective, spreading to form a thick grey band around a bed. Some are too tall to be used as edging plants, except for very large beds, but *A. pontica* is relatively compact, reaching a height of about 30cm (1ft), and producing a carpet of silver-grey filigree foliage.

Divide and multiply The border perennials suggested here will still need dividing after a few years (every third year is about right for most of them). If you don't, the clumps may become congested or too large, and flowering may suffer as a result. If you remove and replant new pieces from around the edges of the clumps (you can discard the old middle sections), you will be able to increase your stock for nothing, and will probably start off with larger plants than you would usually be able to buy. This will enable you to provide more instant results with less effort and the minimum of competition from weeds.

Versatile and charming, the evergreen *Iberis sempervirens* is perfect for providing cover and flowers profusely in late spring.

CONIFERS

Conifers can be ideal low-maintenance plants – the dwarf and slow-growing conifers won't outgrow their welcome, and they come in 'blues', greys and golds as well as greens, and in an impressive array of shapes and outlines – conical, ball-shaped, pencil-like, prostrate, and angled. If used sensibly as part of an overall garden design, they needn't be dull or boring, and they will add a great deal to a low-maintenance garden.

Because they are evergreen, and they seldom if ever need pruning – unless you choose a really rapid grower, such as the Leyland cypress (× *Cupressocyparis leylandii*) – it is easy for the low-maintenance gardener to fall into the trap of planting too many conifers. They work best in a small garden if you choose species and varieties with contrasting shapes and foliage colour, and integrate them carefully into the overall garden design.

Dwarf conifers are popular companions for heathers, but bear in mind that heathers are not quite as labour-saving as you might imagine. The bed will require frequent weeding until the heathers are large enough to carpet the ground; if you fail to clip them over with shears after flowering they can soon become straggly and unattractive, and after a few years it may be necessary to replant the bed.

Siting conifers Try a collection of conifers in an area of paving (just leave planting areas unpaved), or cover the areas between the conifers with gravel. The latter is especially effective because the gravel provides a light background for the conifers, showing them to their best advantage, and weeds – if they appear – can easily be controlled (see p. 23).

The graceful form of *Chamaecyparis pisifera* 'Filifera Aurea', with its golden feathery growth, is a happy choice for appealing low-maintenance cover.

A word of warning – do check that your plants really are dwarf if you want them to remain compact. You need to be especially careful with names – the variety can make a huge difference. *Chamaecyparis lawsoniana* can grow to 10m (30ft) or more, while *C. l.* 'Minima Aurea' probably won't reach much higher than 1m (3ft) in a garden. The words 'Nana', 'Minima' or 'Pygmaea' as part of the name are good indicators of it being a true dwarf.

Some plants that are sold as dwarf conifers may soon outgrow their space – the popular *Chamaecyparis pisifera* 'Boulevard' can reach over 2m (6ft) in less than 10 years, and it is a major effort to dig one out if you've planted it in the wrong place.

Ground cover Prostrate conifers are especially useful for a labour-saving garden. If you plant *Juniperus media* 'Pfitzeriana Aurea', for example, it will make a spreading plant 3.6m (12ft) wide yet no more than 1m (3ft) high in less than 10 years, completely smothering any weeds. This plant is especially attractive in spring, when the new shoots are a lovely yellow. Others, such as *Juniperus horizontalis* 'Bar Harbor' and *J. communis* 'Hornibrookii' (syn. 'Prostrata'), are even more ground-hugging.

If you are grouping conifers together, contrast shapes, colours and textures – perhaps a *Chamaecyparis pisifera* 'Filifera Nana Aurea' (golden thread-like foliage) with *Chamaecyparis obtusa* 'Nana Gracilis' (green shell-shaped sprays).

BULBS

Some bulbs can be short-lived and quite demanding unless you are prepared to discard them and start afresh each season. Others – those that are ideal for a labour-saving garden – will thrive for years and multiply in the process, with the minimum of attention. And, of course, these are the best value for money, because your investment multiplies each year! When planning your garden, do not make the mistake of thinking only in terms of spring-flowering bulbs. There are many excellent summer flowerers and a few that will bring much-valued colour in the autumn. There is no reason why you should have to dismiss bulbs for the low-maintenance garden.

LEFT The delicate blossoms of *Anemone blanda* are shown to good advantage when used as edging in a bed beneath shrubs.

RIGHT Drifts of mixed crocus bulbs in a lawn, and INSET the starry blooms of *Ipheion uniflorum*.

We are using the term 'bulb' loosely here, rather than in its botanical sense, to include bulbs, corms and tubers – in other words those 'storage organs' that you would expect to buy from a bulb merchant.

It is necessary to be strict with yourself when it comes to buying bulbs. Most tulips are out, with the possible exception of a few species that multiply freely, such as the yellow and white *T. tarda*. This is because tulips tend to become diseased if not lifted, and small offset bulbs are produced that may take years to flower well. Also to be avoided are hyacinths, gladioli, and anything either too tender to leave outdoors reliably or that will deteriorate if not lifted each year.

Naturalizing bulbs The best way to use bulbs in a low-maintenance garden is to naturalize them, leaving them to grow and multiply over the years. Most gardeners think first of planting bulbs in the lawn, but you can have drifts of plants such as anemones and winter aconites *(Eranthis hyemalis)* beneath trees or shrubs, and if you have a large or medium-sized garden you can use a variety of bulbs, including the delightful *Fritillaria meleagris*, in a 'wild garden' – an area that you set aside for wild flowers and nature, albeit helped along with a few introductions of your own!

If you have a large expanse of lawn and plant bulbs in one area of it, leaving them to naturalize, you will have a good excuse not to cut the grass until relatively late in the season. Cutting parts short and leaving other areas long will give you the beauty of many wild flowers (including lawn weeds) while the foliage of spring-flowering bulbs dies back. This is the key to successful naturalization: *you must let the foliage die off naturally*, otherwise the bulbs won't thrive and multiply.

Trouble-free summer bulbs, such as the yellow *Allium moly*, the crocosmias, and the autumn-flowering Kaffir lilies *(Schizostylis)* and Jersey lilies *(Nerine bowdenii)*, are attractive in an herbaceous or mixed bed. The nerine will need winter protection in cold areas.

Six to naturalize in lawns
Chionodoxa luciliae, glory of the snow
Colchicum autumnale, autumn crocus
Crocus
Cyclamen coum
Cyclamen neapolitanum
Narcissus, daffodil

Six to naturalize beneath or in front of shrubs
Anemone blanda, and many other species
Eranthis hyemalis, winter aconite
Galanthus nivalis, snowdrop
Ipheion uniflorum, spring starflower
Muscari armeniacum, grape hyacinth
Scilla (Endymion) non-scripta, bluebell

GROUND COVER

Ground cover is an essential part of a low-maintenance garden. Bare soil is an invitation to weeds, and in an ideal low-maintenance garden those parts of the ground not covered by landscaping, such as paving stones or gravel, should be carpeted by weed-suppressing plants. This looks more attractive than bare soil, and it will cut down on weeding, one of the most time-consuming and tedious gardening chores.

There are literally hundreds of good ground cover plants that can be used to carpet the ground around other plants, and it is worth buying a book on ground cover if you want to make the most of this important labour-saving feature.

It's essential to be clear about the types of ground cover plants that are available. Some, such as alchemillas and hostas, give only summer cover, but the foliage usually grows early enough to smother emerging weed seedlings, and they are particularly decorative plants in their own right which makes them a popular choice. If, for aesthetic reasons, you want year-round cover, you'll have to choose an evergreen.

Some evergreens can look less than attractive by the end of winter: lamb's ears *(Stachys byzantina,* syn. *S. lanata)* often looks matted and bedraggled, though its grey, felted leaves look wonderful in summer, and snow-in-summer *(Cerastium tomentosum)* will often form bare patches in winter. If you choose carefully, however, you can select those evergreens that will look good in winter as well as summer, such as elephant ears *(Bergenia),* which often have a purplish colour in winter, and heathers.

Pachysandra terminalis makes excellent ground cover. *Hedera colchica* 'Dentata' continues the carpeting under the trees.

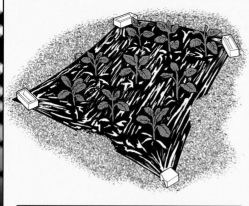

ABOVE LEFT Planting through black polythene to suppress weeds.

LEFT Heathers in winter.

ABOVE Ground cover plants are used to good effect here to soften the border between steps and flowerbeds.

Ground cover design You can use ground cover plants simply to cut down the weeding in beds of conifers or shrubs, or even among herbaceous border plants. And beneath trees, where few plants will grow, ivies can be used to make the ground visually more attractive.

But to use ground cover plants simply to fill in the gaps between other plants is to miss some of their potential. Tough and dependable ground cover plants, with dense but low growth, such as *Pachysandra terminalis* (use the white-splashed 'Variegata' – it's more attractive) and rose of Sharon *(Hypericum calycinum)*, can be used either in beds or in patches on their own, as a design feature. Some of these may prove too invasive to use among other plants, but they are ideal for a narrow bed in front of the house or fence, or perhaps in a rectangle to break up an otherwise dull area of paving. This way of using ground cover as 'texture', like paving or gravel, gives a garden a sense of design, and is an excellent way of having plants without a need for regular maintenance.

Starting problems Plants that will suppress weeds once they are large enough to knit together probably won't be able to compete with them at first. You must start with weed-free ground. If there are deep-rooted perennials, spray the area with a weedkiller that won't persist in the ground, such as those containing glyphosate. Annual weeds can be quickly removed with 'Weedol'. Or you could plant through sheets of black polythene.

PERMANENT PLANTS FOR CONTAINERS

Container gardening is justifiably popular. It enables you to bring colour and interest to parts of the garden that might not otherwise have plants, and a large decorative container can also act as a focal point within the garden. The drawback is that you usually have to plant your containers afresh each spring, and even if you replant again in the autumn they will probably look bare and bleak for the coldest months of the year. Planting them with hardy perennials solves both problems, and in the long term you will probably save money as well as time.

Camellias are a perfect choice for planting in tubs, and their spring blooms are a glorious sight. This one is 'Showgirl'; 'Donation' is also very suitable.

Permanent plantings can be very striking, and there are more possibilities than just shrubs in tubs. Window-boxes filled with perennials are perfectly feasible and can be attractive the year round.

Even hanging baskets have possibilities, though there are major problems with these. Because baskets and other hanging containers contain a relatively small amount of compost and are exposed on all sides, the compost will freeze solid in very cold weather. Winter baskets are sometimes filled with plants such as ivies, but even these are unlikely to last in the long term.

Shrub tubs If you don't have space for many containers, at least make room for a large tub in which to grow a choice shrub. If you want to site specimen plants in a formal area – perhaps you might have a pair flanking your front door – use suitable containers and plants, such as clipped bay trees in white Versailles tubs. In a less formal setting the choice is wide, but opt for evergreens to provide year-round interest.

A camellia should be high on the shopping list; it's easy to give it an acid compost in a container, even if you have an alkaline soil in the garden. The glossy green leaves are always acceptable, but the glory comes in spring, when a well-grown plant will be covered with large flowers long before most other shrubs think of flowering. A dependable and widely available variety, good for tubs and flowering while still young, is 'Donation'. Some rhododendrons also make attractive container shrubs.

It is inevitable that the foliage is an important feature throughout the year, and it's worth going for shrubs with bold or colourful foliage. The golden *Choisya ternata* 'Sundance' will bring life and light to a shady spot all through the year.

Don't dismiss green foliage if it's striking. The bold, hand-like leaves of the false castor oil plant *(Fatsia japonica)* make this a handsome container shrub – in sun or shade.

Window-boxes and troughs Here you can experiment with small shrubs, such as hebes – *H.* × *franciscana* 'Variegata' is a good one – and very dwarf conifers, such as *Juniperus communis* 'Compressa'. And

BELOW Choose evergreen shrubs for really carefree container planting with year-round interest. Here an elegant blending of plants, featuring *Fatsia japonica*, livens up a patio.

there are frequently small specimens of large garden shrubs, including variegated types of *Aucuba japonica*. These can be planted in the garden after a few seasons.

For something a bit different, try a herb window-box, containing perennials such as thyme, chives, and marjoram.

Warning words Containers will require regular watering in dry weather, whatever you grow in them. If you can't meet this commitment, give containers a miss.

LEFT A window-box filled with herbs is both attractive and practical, and makes an interesting addition to an easy-care garden.

LAWNS AND LAWN SUBSTITUTES

Lawns look beautiful if well maintained, but they are among the most labour-intensive features in the garden, and a neglected lawn will detract from the garden rather than enhance it. It may sound like a heresy to some people, but you don't need a lawn to have an attractive garden – there are alternatives that can look just as good and make an equal impact on the garden.

LEFT A small circular lawn can be manageable without too much effort and time; brick edging holds its shape and facilitates mowing.

RIGHT As an alternative to grass, gravel has many advantages. Here it forms the foundation of a small, pretty garden.

Lawns need most attention just when you want more time for yourself, during those warm months when you want to be enjoying the garden rather than working on it. And if you go away for a holiday, you usually come back to long grass that demands cutting quickly.

Paving the garden is one way to avoid the problems associated with lawns, but too much paving can look boring. For a well-designed low-maintenance garden, it's best to have a mixture of surfaces and textures: paving, ground cover, gravel, and if you want grass, keep the lawn small.

It's worth asking yourself what your existing lawns are achieving – what their design function is – and then deciding whether an alternative surface would achieve the same result with less maintenance.

The minimal lawn If you want a lawn as a feature in its own right, then make it small but good, turning it into a focal point. Avoid a simple rectangular lawn set at right angles to the house. If you want a rectangle, try setting it at 45° to the house, or create a circular lawn, perhaps edged with bricks to emphasize the shape and to make mowing easier. If you can, avoid cutting beds into the grass – you will have fewer edges to trim – and keep the area relatively small. If you do this, there will be less to mow and you can spend your time watering, feeding and cutting the grass so that it's a real feature. If you make your lawn large, the chances are that you will neglect it.

The alternatives If your existing lawn is simply there to fill in space, perhaps between paths and drives, consider opting for ground cover plants, such as heathers, pachysandra, and even thyme. They will need much less attention once established, and will look more distinctive than grass.

Don't expect lawn 'alternatives', such as chamomile *(Anthemis nobilis)* or thyme, to be a real substitute for grass. They won't stand the wear, won't give such even cover, and although there's less mowing you will have more hand weeding to do – selective lawn weedkillers are not suitable for this type of 'lawn'.

There is an alternative surface that requires much less maintenance than plants, yet is less harsh and formal than paving. Gravel can be used in place of a lawn, either with flower beds around it like a lawn, or with plants growing through it in special planting areas.

There's a whole range of gravel sizes and colours, and the shades also look different depending on the light and whether they are dry or wet. Use gravel in formal outlines or in flowing lines for a more informal approach. If you lay it on heavy-duty polythene, weeds should not appear, and any that do can be controlled with a yearly application of a path weedkiller, such as 'Pathclear'.

HEDGES AND BOUNDARIES

After lawns, hedges probably represent one of the most unwelcome 'chores' of gardening. Cutting them is often hard, dusty work, and if you have a lot of hedge to cut and it consists of a fast-growing plant like privet, this can be a time-consuming task.

Hedges undoubtedly look better than most fences, especially once they have started to age, and they are a much less expensive option than either walls or fences. You may not need a hedge at all, of course, and, as with the other conventional elements of a garden, it is worth analysing what a hedge is achieving.

Many modern gardens lack the divisions that always used to separate front gardens. 'Open-plan' front gardens are now widespread, while a compromise of simple low walls or post-and-chain dividers is often used to retain the generally open appearance while giving a sense of territory. Even if you wish to create an old-style garden, surrounded by for-mal hedges, it may be possible to reach a compromise that avoids your garden looking out of keeping with others in the area. For example, you might erect a simple chain-link, post-and-rail or post-and-chain divider, but plant a shrub border against it. If you keep to low-growing, and preferably mainly evergreen, shrubs that have a compact habit, your shrub border can double as a 'hedge', whilst taking far less time and effort to maintain.

Hedging need not be abandoned in a low-maintenance scheme. A number of low-growing, compact shrubs are suitable and will largely look after themselves. For a more colourful boundary, lavender is an attractive choice.

24

Post-and-chain dividers can be augmented by the use of an easily maintained shrub hedge – *Berberis thunbergii* is particularly suitable.

Established hedges If you have established hedges, it is probable that you would rather keep them than replace them, even if they need fairly regular trimming.

You can reduce the amount of time spent on trimming by lowering the height of the hedge. Most hedges will tolerate quite severe cutting back, and if you reduce the height of a 1.8m (6ft) hedge by, say, 60cm (2ft), you will have cut the amount of hedge to be trimmed by about 30 per cent, assuming there is about 30cm (1ft) of hedge to trim at the top. There are other benefits in lowering the height of a tall hedge; for example, the top of a 1.2m (4ft) hedge will be much more accessible to cut than the top of a 1.8m (6ft) hedge.

Using a growth inhibitor will cut back the chore even further. 'Cutlass' is a growth regulator that you can spray on in late spring, when you have given your hedge one trim, after which it should keep its shape for the rest of the year. 'Cutlass' is not suitable for box or yew hedges, but can be used on most others.

A new hedge If you are planting a new hedge, make sure that it will remain fairly compact (do *not* plant Leyland cypresses, for example) and that it will require only one cut a year. Avoid privet and shrubby honeysuckle *(Lonicera nitida)* and choose something like *Berberis thunbergii* (green or purple) or *Viburnum tinus* (you'll have winter flowers if you prune in spring).

If you simply want a low boundary marker, the choice is wider, and it is worth considering certain pretty flowering plants, such as lavender or some of the hardier hebes (avoid these in cold areas).

If you want a conifer, the traditional yew is a good choice. It's not as slow-growing in the early years as you might think, but it is easily kept compact with an annual clipping.

AFTERCARE

Even if you have established a labour-saving garden, you will have to undertake some routine tasks if it is to look its best. With planning, and with prompt action when necessary, none of the routine jobs need be onerous, and modern mechanical and chemical aids enable a gardener to keep on top of tasks before they become problems.

LEFT An established scheme combining cover, colour and low upkeep.

ABOVE RIGHT Well-mulched beds and thoughtful planting reap rewards in a delightful mature and fuss-free garden.

RIGHT Use a sprinkler bar to apply weedkillers such as 'Weedol' to beds or a selective weedkiller to lawns.

It is important to get plants established as quickly as possible. The sooner they are growing away vigorously, the more quickly they will look better, cover the ground and compete with weeds. Even if you incorporate plenty of garden compost, 'Forest Bark' Ground and Composted Bark, or other organic material when planting, it won't do any harm to feed your plants every spring. And for the first year, a couple of applications of ICI Liquid Growmore or Miracle-Gro will help enormously, as these fertilizers are suitable for most plants and, being liquid, take effect quickly.

Mulch A mulch is also important – both to retain moisture in the ground and to suppress weeds – and it is worth topping up the mulch each spring or autumn so that it remains deep enough to be effective. Aim for a depth of 5cm (2in). It is unlikely that you will have enough garden compost or rotted manure, but you can use a product like 'Forest Bark' Chipped Bark, which also has the advantage of looking good.

For shrub borders, you can lay black polythene and plant through this (or clear polythene if you cover it with chipped bark or gravel to improve the appearance).

Weeding and watering These are chores that you want to avoid as far as possible; mulching will do much to eliminate both.

It is best to avoid watering, if possible. Unless you water thoroughly, the plant roots may be encouraged to stay near the surface, making them more vulnerable to drought should you stop watering. Your garden will, for the most part, contain established perennials, such as shrubs, and these should be able to fend for themselves unless they have only recently been planted.

If weeds become a problem, it is easy to kill annual and newly-emerging weeds around established plants with 'Weedol', using a sprinkler bar designed for the job. For paths and gravel areas, one application of 'Pathclear' should prevent weeds becoming established.

Lawns Lawns need feeding, and often weeding. You can save effort by using a combined lawn weedkiller and fertilizer, such as 'Lawnsman' Weed & Feed.

Pests and diseases Some plants – for example, roses – will almost certainly need spraying against some pest or disease. It makes sense to use a multi-action product, such as 'Roseclear', which contains an insecticide and a fungicide. Don't be put off by the name – it can also be used on many other shrubs.

If you let pests such as aphids get a hold, they will be more difficult to control. Keep a ready-mixed spray such as a 'Bug Gun!' handy, so that you can treat the pests immediately you notice them without having to bother about mixing a spray.

SIXTY OF THE BEST

It is the plants that make or mar a garden. The shortlist that follows can only be an arbitrary selection, but the plants described here have been chosen because they are both reliable and showy. If you include several of these as a starting point, you can add to them yourself later, but you will have an existing framework of worthy plants. The heights and spreads given are typical after 10 to 15 years in normal garden conditions, but these can vary widely. Some plants, especially the conifers, may grow larger with time.

The attractive berries of the female *Aucuba japonica* 'Variegata'

SHRUBS

Aucuba japonica

Spotted laurel is a tough and adaptable shrub, and is attractive enough for a place in almost any garden. An evergreen, it will tolerate full sun or full shade. The species itself is green and uninteresting, so grow one of the variegated forms such as 'Crotonifolia' or 'Variegata'. The latter doesn't have such good variegation, but as a female plant it may produce red berries as a bonus if there's a male nearby. It is undemanding about soil or site, and has a height and spread of about 1.5m (5ft).

Berberis thunbergii

It is worth making a point of including some deciduous shrubs, otherwise your garden will become predictable and boring. This berberis and its varieties are easy and undemanding. Most attain a height of 1.8m (6ft), with a spread of 1.2m (4ft), and can be used to make an attractive hedge that needs clipping only once a year.

'Atropurpurea' is a bronzy red, 'Aurea' is yellow green, and 'Rose Glow' is purple, mottled with silver and pink. There are many other varieties, including dwarf forms. All will thrive in any soil and will tolerate some shade, though they prefer sun.

Buxus sempervirens

Box is not the dull plant you might think if you grow a variegated type, such as 'Marginata' or 'Aureovariegata'. Boxes do not grow too rapidly; they will eventually attain a height of 2.4m (8ft), with a spread of 1.5m (5ft), but they can be chopped back quite drastically. Provided they are not left to dry out, they make good evergreens for containers, and the green form makes a good low-maintenance hedge. They will grow in most reasonable soils, thriving in chalky areas, either in sun or in partial shade.

Camellia 'Donation'

Choisya ternata 'Sundance'

Camellia 'Donation'

One of the best of the flowering evergreens, this variety is perhaps the best camellia to grow if you have space for only one in your garden or patio. The large pink double flowers, appearing in spring, are set against thick, glossy dark-green leaves. Attaining a height of some 1.8m (6ft), with a spread of 1.5m (5ft), this camellia is best placed in partial shade, sheltered from cold north and east winds. A peaty, acid soil is required for the most successful results, but if you have chalky soil you can grow it in a large tub filled with more suitable soil.

Choisya ternata 'Sundance'

The green form of Mexican orange blossom is an attractive evergreen with very fragrant white flowers appearing in May, often with a second flowering later. 'Sundance' is a yellow-leaved variety that will lighten a dull area throughout the year. Choisya requires a well-drained soil, but will grow successfully in sun or partial shade. It grows best in a position sheltered from wind, and reaches a height and spread of some 1.5m (5ft) each way.

Erica carnea (syn. E. herbacea)

Heathers need no introduction, being one of the most popular dwarf evergreens due to their carpeting habit, their general resilience, and their provision of colour and interest in the garden when much else is dormant. There are many varieties, most of them pink or white, flowering in winter or early spring. 'Springwood White' and the carmine 'King George' are particularly good varieties. Most heaths and heathers prefer an acid soil, but this winter- and spring-flowering species is reasonably lime tolerant, though you should not place it in a shallow chalk soil. *Erica carnea* grows best in sun, though it can tolerate partial shade; it reaches a height of some 30cm (1ft), with a spread of 60cm (2ft).

Hebe × *franciscana* 'Variegata' is a versatile compact shrub

Hypericum calycinum

Fatsia japonica

Known as the false castor oil plant, this is an evergreen foliage plant with big palmate leaves. Mature plants have white ball-shaped flower heads in late autumn. Fatsia will grow in sun or partial shade, reaching a height of 1.8m (6ft), with a spread of 1.5m (5ft), but in cold areas it prefers a sheltered position. It will grow in any good garden soil.

Hebe × franciscana 'Variegata'

A compact foliage plant with small green and cream evergreen leaves, this is useful at the front of a border, as an edging, or in window-boxes or tubs. It will tolerate most soils if well drained, and will grow in sun or partial shade, but it is best avoided in very cold areas. This hebe reaches a height of some 45cm (1½ft), with a spread of 60cm (2ft).

Hypericum calycinum

The rose of Sharon is tough and very bright in flower, at which time it is a mass of large bright yellow blooms with prominent stamens. Evergreen, or almost evergreen, this plant will thrive in sun or shade, on almost any soil, including shallow chalk soils. It reaches a height of 30cm (1ft) and spreads indefinitely, so it is not suitable for mixed beds, but it looks most attractive when planted in blocks or areas confined by walls or paths.

Iberis sempervirens

Perennial candytuft is a dwarf evergreen shrub, suitable for the rock garden, the front of a border, or crevices at the edge of a path. The tight green mounds, some 23cm (9in) high, with a spread of 60cm (2ft), are covered with white flowers in May and June. If you want a very low form, grow 'Little Gem' (10cm/4in). Growing best in sun, this plant requires a well-drained position and thrives on poor soils.

Laurus nobilis

Sweet bay is popular in herb gardens, but it is also an excellent formal tub plant, especially if clipped to shape. Although it can be grown in the border, it is best used as an isolated specimen. Sweet bay will grow in any well-drained, ordinary garden soil, but it needs a sunny, sheltered position. The leaves may be damaged in a harsh winter, but the plant often recovers. A height of 1.8m (6ft), with a spread of 90cm (3ft), is normal, but mature border plants can be much larger.

Pachysandra terminalis 'Variegata'

Japanese spurge has insignificant flowers, but the plant produces a uniform carpet of white and green foliage and thrives even in the shade of trees. It is best planted in bold drifts as ground cover, and will grow in any normal garden soil, preferring partial shade.

Rosa 'Ballerina'

Most modern roses are unsuitable for a labour-saving garden, but some hybrid shrub roses are well worth growing. This is a good one to start with, having large clusters of small single pink and white flowers that are also fragrant. Reaching a height of about 1.2m (4ft), with a spread of 1m (3ft), it has bright green glossy leaves. Other roses worth considering are mentioned on p.10. The best results will come from a fertile soil and a sunny position.

Rosa 'Ballerina', an ideal low-maintenance choice

Viburnum tinus

Laurustinus is an evergreen that can look a little dull in the summer, with its quite large dark-green leaves, but it is always a well-clothed and well-shaped plant. Laurustinus comes into its own from November onwards, and usually carries its clusters of white or pink flowers through to March and beyond. This shrub will grow well in most soils, even on chalk, in sun or shade, reaching a height of 2.4m (8ft), with a spread of 1.2m (4ft).

Viburnum tinus 'Gwenllian'

Yucca filamentosa

Adam's needle is a fine 'architectural' plant, useful as a focal point in the summer when it's in flower. The rosette of large, sword-shaped evergreen leaves can be a feature in its own right, especially in the variety 'Variegata', but the crowning glory is the big, bold spike of huge white bell-shaped flowers. This dramatic plant should do well in any ordinary soil, provided it is well drained, and will thrive in sun or partial shade. In flower, it reaches a height of 1.5m (5ft), with a spread of 1m (3ft).

Yucca filamentosa 'Variegata'

CONIFERS

Most conifers are suitable for a low-maintenance garden, and the dwarf conifers can be used in place of broad-leaved shrubs, which often require regular pruning and may be more vulnerable to pests. Those suggested below are only a selection, representing the diversity of dwarf conifers. Most of those listed are undemanding about soil, and will thrive in sun or partial shade, unless otherwise stated.

Chamaecyparis lawsoniana 'Minima Aurea'

A very slow-growing plant, this has tightly-packed yellow foliage, form-

Chamaecyparis lawsoniana 'Minima Aurea'

Chamaecyparis pisifera 'Boulevard'

Juniperus communis 'Compressa'

ing a neat cone shape. It is ideal for a heather garden or a large rock garden, reaching a height of 60cm (2ft), with a spread of 45cm (1½ft).

Chamaecyparis obtusa 'Nana Gracilis'

This is a good conifer to grow for a contrast in foliage shape. The dark-green leaves grow in shell-shaped sprays, making it one of the more distinctive green dwarf conifers, and it tends to make a conical bush as it matures. It has a height of 1m (3ft), with a spread of 75cm (2½ft).

Chamaecyparis pisifera 'Boulevard'

One of the most popular and widely available 'blue' conifers, this makes a pyramid-shaped bush, and is quicker-growing than is often assumed. In fact, it can soon become a rather large 'dwarf', reaching a height of 1.8m (6ft), with a spread of 1.2m (4ft). It is more demanding about soil than many conifers, not liking very dry conditions or heavy clay, and it is generally unwise to

attempt to grow this conifer on a very alkaline soil.

Chamaecyparis pisifera 'Filifera Nana Aurea'

This is a good plant to choose to represent those with thin, thread-like foliage. It makes a loose mound of distinctive yellow foliage, reaching a height and spread of about 1m (3ft) each way and offering a good contrast in shape, colour and texture to most other conifers. It is not very demanding, but avoid very dry soils or very alkaline ground.

Juniperus communis 'Compressa'

This represents the real miniatures, reaching a height of 45cm (1½ft), with a spread of 23cm (9in). It makes a narrow, upright cone, and is quite at home in a window-box or a sink garden. If you plant it among the larger conifers, it will be unable to compete for attention, but in the right place it's a real gem. 'Compressa' will grow on most soils, including shallow chalk, but it must be given a sunny position.

The elegant *Juniperus* × *media* 'Pfitzeriana Aurea'

Juniperus communis 'Hornibrookii'

The shoots of this prostrate conifer are green when young, but later often turn bronze. This plant is a good choice if you want a conifer as ground cover, because it forms a prostrate mat that creeps over low obstacles, reaching a height of 30cm (1ft), but spreading up to 2.1m (7ft).

Juniperus horizontalis 'Bar Harbor'

Another example of a carpeting juniper, this is only some 15cm (6in) high, but will spread to 1.5m (5ft), creeping over the ground and smothering weeds. The foliage is grey-blue in summer, but turns almost mauve in winter. Plant in full sun for the best effect.

Juniperus × *media* 'Pfitzeriana Aurea'

This is one to try if you want a weed-smotherer with much more height than the carpeting type of conifer. The branches grow almost horizontally, but on a much more upright plant than the previous two conifers. In time it makes a large, spreading plant 1m (3ft) high, but spreading over some 3.6m (12ft). The golden colouring is at its best on new shoots in spring and early summer, but this is a bright plant all year round. An undemanding conifer, it thrives in full sun or partial shade.

Juniperus scopulorum 'Skyrocket'

There are several good fastigiate (narrow, upright) conifers, including *J. communis* 'Hibernica', but 'Skyrocket' is perhaps the most popular. It grows into a very narrow upright column of blue-grey foliage, making a good accent plant where the garden lacks height. This is one of the few tallish conifers suitable for a small garden, reaching a height of 3m (10ft) and a spread of 60cm (2ft).

Taxus baccata 'Fastigiata Aurea'

This golden form of the Irish yew will make a narrow upright column, reaching a height of 1.8m (6ft), with a spread of 60cm (2ft). *T. b.* 'Standishii' is similar but slower-growing

Acanthus spinosus is a distinctive border plant

and smaller – take your pick according to whether you want slow growth or a faster and taller plant.

HERBACEOUS BORDER PLANTS

The heights given are approximate flowering heights in typical garden conditions. They may vary depending on soil and site, and some plants with tall flower spikes may be much shorter when not in flower.

Acanthus spinosus
Although dull – white or purple – in colour, the hooded flowers of bear's breeches are very striking on their tall, stiff spikes. This is also worth growing for foliage as well as flowers. The large radiating leaves with their long, stiff spines produce a bold clump of foliage that makes this an eye-catching plant. Bear's breeches reaches a height of 1.2m (4ft), with a spread of 90cm (3ft).

Ajuga reptans
Bugle is a fairly rampant carpeter, but useful for ground cover at the front of a border, reaching a height of only 15cm (6in) but spreading up to 60cm (2ft). There are short upright spikes, usually of blue flowers, in late spring and early summer, but bugle is grown primarily as a foliage plant. 'Purpurea' has reddish-purple leaves; 'Multicolor' (also sold as 'Rainbow') is mottled bronze, pink and yellow; 'Variegata' is cream and green, and there are other worthwhile varieties.

Anemone × hybrida
You may find Japanese anemones listed as varieties of *A. japonica* or *A. hupehensis*, and there are several good named varieties, all reaching a height of 90cm (3ft), with a spread of 60cm (2ft). The flowers, usually pink or white, double or single, are about 5cm (2in) across and carried on long wiry stems from late summer onwards. They will grow on most soils, and even thrive on shallow chalk soils. Although sun is tolerated, they are particularly useful for lightly shaded areas.

Astilbe hybrids

You may find these listed as varieties of *A. × arendsii*, but more commonly they are sold under their varietal name. The foliage is quite feathery in appearance, and bronze in some varieties, making these acceptable plants even when not in flower. But the main attraction lies in the bright and bold 'plumes' of red, pink or white flowers, appearing from early to late summer. Astilbes need a moist soil, and they are best avoided in very dry areas. They will thrive in full sun, but generally put in a bright and commendable show in partial shade. They have a height of 60cm (2ft) and a spread of 45cm (1½ft).

Bergenia cordifolia

Also known as elephant ears, this is one of the most important plants for a labour-saving garden. It's an excellent ground cover plant, evergreen, quite colourful in winter, when the big, heart-shaped leaves often turn purplish, and sports bright, showy pink flowers in spring. The height, in flower, is about 45cm (1½ft), with a spread of some 60cm (2ft). Try growing some of the named varieties and other species of bergenia. Although these plants do best in moist ground, they will put in a respectable performance on dry soils, and they can be depended upon in full sun or partial shade.

Convallaria majalis

Lily-of-the-valley has something of a reputation for being rather difficult to grow, but really it's just a matter of leaving it alone to become established and form a carpeting colony of plants about 23cm (9in) high, spreading by stoloniferous roots. This plant is not a good choice for the border, but it is well suited to a wild garden or a cool shady position. It is best known for its small nodding white bell flowers and wonderful fragrance, but if you can obtain a form with variegated foliage you will have a very desirable plant indeed. Enrich the soil with plenty of humus-forming material (such as garden compost or 'Forest Bark' Ground and Composted Bark soil conditioner) when planting. Lilies-of-the-valley require a moist soil, and benefit from an annual mulch.

The invaluable spring-flowering *Bergenia cordifolia*

Convallaria majalis 'Albolineata' is a pretty carpeting plant

Cortaderia selloana

The pampas grass, with its white or silvery plumes in late summer and autumn, is rarely used for a mixed border unless it's very big, in which case it will provide height at the back. In a labour-saving garden, however, it is more likely to be used as a specimen plant to act as a focal point. This evergreen perennial grass can be huge – 2.4m (8ft) is not uncommon, and a large clump can be almost the same across – but a compact variety, such as 'Pumila', is more suitable for a small garden. Pampas grass thrives in well-drained soil in full sun, but will grow in most soils and in partial shade.

Erigeron

Fleabane is not as widely grown as it deserves to be. The flowers look like Michaelmas daisies, but on very compact plants, with a height of 45cm (1½ft), and a spread of 60cm (2ft). The colours are mainly shades of blue or pink, and there are named varieties. Fleabane is undemanding about soil, but not happy in very dry conditions, though it likes full sun.

Erigeron 'Darkest of All'

Helleborus

Both the Christmas rose *(H. niger)* and the Lenten rose *(H. orientalis)* are trouble-free if left to multiply, and they flower between Christmas and Easter. Both have a height of 30cm (1ft), with a spread of 45cm (1½ft), and will grow in shade or partial shade, in most soils, including shallow chalk soils. They prefer humus in the soil, however, and do not like it too dry.

Hemerocallis

The individual trumpet-shaped flowers last little more than a day, hence the common name of day lily, but there is a succession of them over a long period throughout the summer. There are many named varieties, in shades of yellow, orange, red and pink, all with the same large, strap-shaped leaves. In flower, they have a height of 75cm (2½ft) and a spread of 60cm (2ft).

Hostas

Hostas, sometimes known as plantain lilies, have become some of the most popular foliage plants. There are dozens of widely available species and varieties, and many more are available from specialists. They are best in shade or partial shade, though some can also be grown successfully in full sun. They are undemanding about the soil, but will do much better if the ground is moist. Although the leaves die down in the autumn, hostas are nevertheless good ground cover plants, provided perennial weeds are cleared first. The large and prolific foliage shuts out the light from other weeds that may try to become established.

Hostas come with foliage in many shapes and sizes – some are almost blue; others are yellow, and many are very attractively variegated. Typical garden varieties have a height ranging between 30 and 60cm (1 and 2ft), with a spread of 60cm (2ft), but some rock-garden hostas may be only half this height, while others, such as *H. sieboldiana* 'Elegans', can reach 90cm (3ft) or more. The only real problem with hostas is damage caused by slugs and snails, which often attack the developing leaves in spring and mar the foliage. Consider using a slug killer in spring if slugs are a problem in your garden.

Hemerocallis 'Burning Daylight'
BELOW *Hosta fortunei* 'Albopicta'

Kniphofia

Red hot pokers take a year or two to settle down and make an imposing clump, but then they should thrive for years with the minimum of attention, though in cold districts it is worth protecting the crowns with straw or bracken during the winter. There are some charming small species, but for sheer impact the large hybrids are usually grown, the red, orange or yellow flowers atop tall, stiff spikes that can reach a height of

Liriope muscari

Pulmonaria 'Leopard'

some 1.5m (5ft). The strap-like foliage is not unattractive even when the plant is out of flower. Kniphofias should be grown in full sun, and in a well-drained soil to avoid winter losses.

Liriope muscari
Out of flower, the grass-like foliage of lilytuft is not very interesting, but the plant is easy to grow, even in unpromising places, and it flowers in early to late autumn, when most other flowers are past their best. The blue flower spikes resemble tall grape hyacinths. They do best in a light, acid to neutral soil, though they can succeed on chalky ground. With a height of 45cm (1½ft) and a spread of 30cm (1ft), lilytufts are particularly useful for partial shade.

Nepeta mussinii
Especially useful because it combines pleasing flowers with aromatic grey-green foliage, catmint holds

interest before and after flowering. It will grow in any ordinary soil, provided this is reasonably well drained, reaching a height and spread of some 60cm (2ft) each way. Although it will grow in partial shade, the plants are better in full sun. There is confusion between this species and *N.* × *faassenii*, and one is sometimes distributed as the other; this doesn't matter from a gardening viewpoint, as both are fine plants.

Pulmonaria
Lungwort is very useful as a ground cover for shady areas, and charming early in spring, when the blue or pink-and-blue flowers appear. There are several good species, *P. officinalis* being the most popular, and varieties, many of which have silvery markings or spots on the foliage. Lungworts prefer moist ground and succeed in partial or full shade. They reach a height of 30cm (1ft), with a spread of 60cm (2ft).

The sunny blooms of *Rudbeckia deamii*, black-eyed Susan

Rudbeckia deamii
You might find this plant, commonly known as black-eyed Susan, listed as *R. fulgida deamii*. This species is just one of many good perennial rudbeckias, which help to provide interest in the border from midsummer to early autumn or later. The flowers are large, with bright-yellow petals around a dark central cone. Undemanding of soil, but best in full sun, the plant has a height and spread of 60cm (2ft).

Sedum spectabile
The ice plant is one of those perennials that you'll have in the garden for years once it is established, and you will be delighted by its presence. The succulent greyish foliage make this a compact and attractive plant from the moment it emerges in spring, and the season is rounded off with one of the best displays of all autumn border plants. The flattish attractive pink or red flower heads are long-lasting, and they bring the bonus of lots of butterflies, which seem to love the plant. There are several good named varieties and hybrids. Heights vary from 30 to 60cm (1-2ft) and plants spread to about 45cm (1½ft).

Sidalcea malviflora
This plant is not very widely grown, but it is undemanding if left undisturbed, and will provide some height without the need for staking, except in a very exposed position. Spikes of pink flowers resemble miniature hollyhocks, over a clump of low-growing basal leaves. Any ordinary soil is suitable, and they will tolerate some shade although they prefer full sun. In flower, they reach a height of 75cm (2½ft), with a spread of up to 45cm (1½ft).

Trandescantia virginiana
Sometimes known as either spiderwort or trinity flower, the varieties grown are hybrids of *T. virginiana* or *T. × andersoniana*. They are not the most striking border plants – there is rather a lot of leaf in relation to flower – but they are dependable and demand little attention. They often attract insects with their clusters of three-petalled flowers about 2.5cm (1in) across. These come in shades of blue, purple, rose or white, according to variety. Any ordinary, well-drained soil is suitable, and they will be happy in full sun or partial shade. They reach a height and spread of 60cm (2ft).

Veronica spicata

This has not been chosen for inclusion because it is among the brightest or most colourful border plants, but because it can be relied upon to grow and to thrive, largely unattended, for many years. The plant makes a compact clump of dark-green leaves, with short spikes of blue flowers in middle and late summer. There are also white and pink varieties, and all will grow in most soils, though they do best where there is plenty of humus. Although they will grow well in partial shade, they thrive in full sun. They reach a height of 45cm (1½ft), with a spread of 30cm (1ft).

Chionodoxa luciliae 'Pink Giant'

BULBS

Unless otherwise stated, all the bulbs here will do well in any normal garden soil, and most will do very well even on chalky soils. The only soils that bulbs do not generally tolerate are those that are likely to become waterlogged in winter. The spreads given for the bulbs below should be taken only as a very approximate guide after several years of growth. Many will form increasingly large clumps as they grow and divide naturally, forming clusters of separate plants rather than large individuals.

Anemone blanda 'Alba'

Anemone blanda

Also known as wind flowers, these spring carpeters can be disappointing at first – newly-planted tubers often flower poorly – but if you leave them undisturbed they will carpet the ground in time. Use them to bring patches of early colour to the herbaceous border, to carpet among deciduous shrubs, or to naturalize in short grass around a deciduous tree. The flowers, which resemble large single daises and come in shades of blue, pink or white, will cover an established clump in spring. A well-grown clump has a height of 10cm (4in) with a spread of 30cm (1ft).

Chionodoxa luciliae

Glory of the snow is one of the welcome sights of early spring. The blue-and-white starry flowers put in a surprisingly bright display for such a small and frail-looking plant. Naturalize them in short grass or plant them among low-growing plants like heathers. They do best in full sun but still put in a good performance in light shade, reaching a height of 15cm (6in), with a spread of 10cm (4in).

43

Crocosmia 'Ember Glow'

Colchicum autumnale

Colchicum autumnale

This is just one of several species of so-called autumn crocuses, all of which are worth trying. They are not true crocuses, but the flowers resemble huge crocuses and appear when little else is achieving a respectable show of flowers. The large leaves appear in spring and far exceed the flowering height of 15cm (6in). Plant the bulbs in groups in the border, in front of shrubs, or beneath deciduous trees if the soil is not too dry. If they are left undisturbed, they will form large and spectacular clumps after a few years. Pink is the main colour, but there are also lilac and white forms.

Crocosmia

These are often confused with montbretias, to which they are closely related. *C. masonorum* is a robust and hardy choice (some crocosmias are not suitable for very cold areas). The arching sprays of brilliant orange-scarlet flowers bloom in mid-summer, over a bunch of strap-shaped leaves, giving the clump a height and spread of some 60cm (2ft) each way. You will often find crocosmias and montbretias sold as growing plants, along with the ordinary herbaceous perennials, but you can also buy the corms from bulb suppliers.

Crocus

The popular spring-flowering crocus needs no introduction. The small species, such as *C. chrysanthus*, flower very early, but the large-flowered Dutch type is the best choice for a bold naturalized display. This has a flowering height of 10cm (4in), forming established clumps with a spread of some 23cm (9in). You can leave these to form pockets of colour in the border, but they are especially attractive in grass, and will even naturalize well beneath some deciduous trees, such as silver birch.

Cyclamen

The dwarf hardy cyclamen, which have a height of 10cm (4in), with a spread of 23cm (9in), lack the showy display of many of the larger bulbs, but some of them are very useful because they can be naturalized to give an autumn display in shade, often beneath large trees. *C. hederifolium* (syn. *C. neapolitanum)* has pink flowers in early and mid-autumn (there is also a white form), and attractively variegated leaves. Try following this with *C. coum*, a species that bears deep crimson, carmine, magenta or white flowers from early winter into early spring. They prefer a humus-rich soil, perhaps with leafmould, and take a season or two to become established.

Eranthis hyemalis

Winter aconite is another plant that may prove a little difficult to establish, seldom flowering well at first, but thriving and flowering prolifically once it has been allowed to naturalize. Try it in short grass beneath trees, or among shrubs. The bright yellow flowers, resembling large buttercups with a green ruff behind the petals, are particularly welcome because they flower in late winter and early spring. They require a humus-rich soil to do really well, and prefer partial shade, spreading in time to form a clump some 23cm (9in) across, with a flowering height of 8cm (3in).

Fritillaria meleagris

Snakeshead fritillary is a delicate-looking plant, but it does surprisingly well if left to naturalize in a wild garden, in grass, or even in clumps in the border in front of shrubs. The nodding pink, purple or white bell flowers have an interesting chequer pattern. Fritillaries will flourish in sun or partial shade, reaching a flowering height of 30cm (1ft), with a spread of 23cm (9in), but they are unlikely to do well in very dry soils.

Galanthus nivalis

Snowdrops can prove disappointing because they take time to settle down and produce large clumps. If you can leave them undisturbed, however, they will reward you with one of the most pleasing sights of late winter and early spring, forming clumps of flowers with a height of 15cm (6in) and spread of 23cm (9in). There are many varieties, all with nodding white bells, and you can also buy double ones. Snowdrops are best in woodland conditions, in a leafy soil, but can be successful when grown in clumps in the border or in front of shrubs.

Eranthis hyemalis brings colour to the garden in late winter

45

Narcissus bulbocodium is a good bulb for naturalizing

Ipheion uniflorum

A border of this charming spring-flowering bulb will eventually form a delightful ribbon of blue upward-facing star-like flowers, some 10cm (4in) high. They can also be used to make a carpet between herbaceous plants or shrubs. They multiply freely, making good clumps within just a few years, and are happy in sun or partial shade.

Muscari armeniacum

Tough, dependable and showy, grape hyacinths are cheap to buy and quick to multiply, producing masses of short stiff spikes clustered with small blue flowers. Grow them as an edging, in drifts beneath or in front of shrubs, or simply as clumps in a border or rock garden. Undemanding about soil, and happy in sun or partial shade, the clumps have a flowering height and spread of about 23cm (9in).

Narcissi

There are so many good narcissi – a group which includes the trumpet daffodils – that they could be the subject of a whole book. They are good value, too, naturalizing easily and multiplying freely. The large-flowered type are best for naturalizing, though some of the tiny species, such as *N. bulbocodium*, can naturalize very successfully in grass. Heights vary from about 5cm (2in) to about 60cm (2ft), with clumps that spread in proportion with age. Very large clumps are best divided and replanted to encourage them to keep flowering at full strength.

Nerine bowdenii

This is not a plant for cold areas, but in mild districts it should do well. If in doubt, give nerines a little winter protection by placing dry straw or leaves over the bulbs, keeping the covering in place with netting. The

Nerine bowdenii

Schizostylis coccinea

nerine is one of the finest autumn-flowering plants in the garden, and seen at its best if left undisturbed, which makes it ideal for a low-maintenance scheme. Try planting a small bed by the house in the front garden with nothing but nerines. A small narrow bed won't detract from the garden when there are no flowers, but you will have a really eye-catching display in late autumn. Nerines have a flowering height of 45cm (1½ft), with a spread of 30cm (1ft), and thrive in well-drained soil in a sunny position.

Schizostylis coccinea
The Kaffir lily is another autumn-flowering bulb, useful for extending the season of colour, and is easy to grow, provided the soil is not too dry. It is not hardy in very cold areas, but should come through most winters without protection in mild areas. The loose spikes of pink or red flowers, some 60cm (2ft) high, are carried over sword-shaped foliage that spreads to 30cm (1ft). Try planting clumps in a mixed border, and leave the bulbs undisturbed to multiply.

Scilla non-scripta
You are likely to find bluebells sold under one of their other names – *Endymion non-scripta* – but whatever the name, this popular flower needs no introduction. Those sold by bulb merchants are improved forms of the wild bluebell, with bigger flowers, and available in shades of pink and in white as well as blue. These have a height and spread of about 30cm (1ft) each way. As anyone who has admired bluebells in their natural woodland setting will know, they can carpet a shady area very successfully if left to get on with the job of multiplying. This makes them ideal for the wild garden, or for the ground in front of shrubs.

INDEX AND ACKNOWLEDGEMENTS

Page numbers in **bold type** indicate illustrations

Picture credits

Gillian Beckett: 7(c), 9(cl), 12(t).
Derek Gould: 27.
Peter McHoy: 10, 11(t), 14, 18, 22, 23, 25, 30, 31(tr), 32(t), 34(t,c,b), 35(tr), 38, 39 (t,cr), 42, 44(tr).
S. & O. Mathews: 26.
Harry Smith Horticultural Collection: 1, 4-5, 6, 7(tr,b), 8, 9(b), 11(c), 12(b), 13, 15(t,cr), 16, 17(inset), 20, 21(t), 31(tl), 36, 40(cr), 41(tl), 43(cr), 45, 47 (bl).
Michael Warren: 17, 19 (tr,cl), 21(b), 24, 28-29, 32(cl), 33, 35(tl), 37, 40(tr), 41(tr), 43(tr), 44(tl), 46, 47(tl).

Artwork by Simon Roulstone

48